So you want to be a full-time guitar tutor?

Also by Al Summers

Modebusters' Handbook
"remarkable...amazing"
(*Guitar Techniques* magazine)

Circles & Cycles for Musicians
"incredibly informative"
(*Guitar Techniques* magazine)

Theory Dictionary for guitar players
"excellent & informative"
(*Total Guitar*)

Wacko Modes & how to make your own

Don't be afraid of the neck

New progressive arpeggio-based pieces
for fingerstyle or plectrum

Acoustic (progressive) Fingerpicking tunes

So you want to be a full-time guitar tutor?

Al Summers

Luniver Press

Published in 2006 by Luniver Press

Luniver Press
Beckington, BA11 6TT, United Kingdom
www.luniver.com

British Library Cataloguing in Publication Data
A catalog record is available from the British Library

Library of Congress Cataloguing in Publication Data
A catalog record is available from the Library of Congress

ISBN-13: 978-1-905986-02-6
ISBN-10: 1-905986-02-5

Table of Contents

There was to be a fine quotation at this point, but there are so many fine quotations, even if I had narrowed down my choice to just one guitar teacher (who would most probably have been Fernando Sor). Limiting myself to just a page would have tested the editor in me too greatly[1].

A page of inspiring, insightful Sor comments might have been simple enough but I would have soon wanted to include relevant wisdoms from further afield: other instruments; other arts; and many other disciplines.

There is hardly a subject that cannot inform us in some way to make us better tutors: the only limitation is closing our minds.

This is a small, humble publication, much of which cannot pretend to be in any way original. It should therefore be dedicated to the generations of guitar teachers whose shoulders we stand on, but I'd prefer to dedicate it to one person.

If there is stuff worth knowing in this little book then it is almost certainly down to him in some way; any short-fallings are mine.

to **David Stanley**
what you taught me 30 years ago was inspiring; the way you taught me has enabled me to build on it every day since. Thank you David

Al Summers November 2006

---

[1] I've written the main body of the text in a fairly conversational style: as you read try to let this remind you that teaching should make learning enjoyable and full of vitality, leaving a student with a hunger for more while they are having fun with all the tough, rewarding work that goes with studying this instrument and its music. Balance formality and fun.

THE BRIEF: CONSIDERATIONS

Maybe you've yet to give your first lesson; maybe you've been teaching part-time for some while and are thinking about 'giving up the day-job'.

Do you REALLY want to be a full-time guitar tutor?

The first question I usually ask someone expressing this wish may seem irritating but, if someone older and wiser hadn't asked me a similar question at an early stage, I probably would have ended up pursuing, then finally hating and jacking in a career giving guitar and/or lute recitals. Consider what you think you'd LIKE to do - day in day out.

For me it is and always has been teaching, above everything else. Even when you do what you prefer all day, every job has its trials!

Can you cope cheerfully with: being ruled by a diary that other people don't always remember, leaving you sitting like a lemon waiting for a student who "forgot because I had to wash my hair"; eating and sleeping when you *can* rather than when you are hungry or tired; teaching at break-neck speed with someone who is 'on a roll', soaking up learning like a sponge, then grinding to a snail's pace with infinite patience at the next lesson for a student who finds it hard but is determined to master this delightful and illogical instrument? Have you an endless supply of self-motivation, energetic enthusiasm and a genuine bottomless store of encouragement? Are you the sort of person who looks at the bigger picture?

People say "it must be nice playing guitar all day" – it must be: no successful guitar teacher I know experiences it! I've known 10-hour teaching days when I haven't picked up my own instrument once.

Teaching music as an easy route to a fast and juicy income while getting to practice music of your choice is not going to work out. If you believe it will, look for another career.

Great players don't automatically, perhaps even rarely, make great (or even adequate) tutors, nor necessarily enjoy it.

If you're not the fastest player in town it doesn't mean you won't make a great tutor. Could you answer those bold questions on page eight positively? Yes? Then this might be for you. Try teaching friends or relatives to get a feel for it (if you haven't already) and find out how it feels.

Whatever you decide, think practically: the music industry is huge. The visible jobs are usually only the tip of the iceberg. The job you might end up doing/enjoying may be one you haven't even heard of yet. So aim at some things you know might be possible rather than setting hopes on one thing of which you've no real experience. Don't tunnel your vision too early on. Most of us end up specializing to some degree at least. The aim of course is to end up doing what you're best at, and maybe what you enjoy most, in your field.

For those who have no history of work yet, get some real world experience before heading for full-time music tuition. You can always teach on a part-time basis. You will relate better to students and have better teaching psychology having had some experience. Straight out of school, to college or university then into teaching is a great way of alienating yourself from those everyday folk you'll be trying to tutor.

Immediate steps: learn many different types/styles of music; learn to read music fluently, including a second instrument (keyboard skills are useful – essential for some college courses); study theory; study for some relevant exams; get as much practical experience as you can, and practice! NB Are you taking or have you got GCSE or A level music? Don't worry if not, but make sure your studies at least cover similar ground (you'll need to be able talk to your students and your colleagues on a level using common terms of reference).

A tutor isn't someone who shows students where to put their fingers; it's a much more subtle and interesting task than that and includes: guidance; giving permission (to be creative, to 'let rip' sometimes, to play at full ability, often just to try something); confidence-building/boosting; research tips; the encouragement of understanding over memorizing; energy, enthusiasm and communication; NLP (if you're not sure, look it up: that's not me being rude, it's me being a good tutor – think about it); learning how students learn.

Where will you teach? If you do already, will it be adequate for a full-time professional? At home has obvious advantages but you will never be able to be out of the office *and,* at home, students will know where you live, expect you to be there and available for them. Premises away from home will cost more. There are pros and cons for both situations, many of which will be peculiar to your circumstances: weigh them up and take care not to enter into an arrangement you can't undo simply. See page 22 onwards.

Do you want to be truly full-time? Or will you have other income, as many tutors do, (either in or out of the music industry). Many people assume that you can't possibly earn a living just teaching. I'm not the only private tutor who has been asked at the final lesson of a 90-hour week "what do you actually do for a living then?"..."what else do you do?" is another common question!

Balance and commitment are tricky issues. I have plenty of the latter but am no expert on the former so can't pretend that this booklet will always preach what I practice!

Do you wish to teach one-to-one (the most effective way) or in groups, or combine the two? If you're interested in schools or other institutions see the chapter called Back-to-Back Breadwinning.

Your local area: is there a big enough population? Are there any other tutors or music shops to help you find out if there is a market for you and your business to thrive or survive? The Registry of Guitar Tutors has a list of registered tutors which could help you, and ensure you don't accidentally set up business next door to the established guitar guru if you're moving to a new area to start business! There are other tutor lists on the web too as well as a few teachers who advertise in phone directories. Any contact that genuine tutors have with each other has to benefit the tutors, their students as well as the business and practice of music as a whole.

BASICS AND PRINCIPLES

Teach to be redundant: nurture independent musicians, not clones and parrots. One day your students should become musicians in their own right if you do your job properly. Some of them will become professionals, possibly while you are still teaching them. Set your students off onto a healthy life where music is a source of pleasure, satisfaction — and perhaps income. Try to ensure that music doesn't end up a burden or a source of pain. Deal with posture at an early stage; sometimes this can be done by just keeping an eye, checking small issues and teaching using good principles, easier if you are the tutor who starts a student from scratch.

Problems with posture can sometimes walk through your door if a student has been teaching themselves for a time or had an unaddressed problem: these situations may require gentle progress and continuing patience. As with all subjects you handle in lessons, teach understanding and why, not what and how.

It is a very old adage that best performers do not always or necessarily make the best tutors; great tutors are often not the best performers. You'll possibly have heard this before and will again. Many believe that great players are bound to have the best advice and the best understanding about how to pass it on. Nadia Boulanger was perhaps the best tutor of composers in the twentieth century: how many people know her work?

This is now also beginning to be more acknowledged at higher academic levels, as an article about teaching diplomas in London College of Music's *Forte* magazine made clear early in 2006.

So: what makes a good guitar teacher? Some of the

qualities are almost intangible but a brief look at the more definitive and obvious attributes of good tuition (and a briefer glance at those of the poorer or reluctant members of the teaching profession) might be a half decent idea at this point.

Qualities in best tutors I've known and the most successful ones I've taught: serious about the job; enthusiastic, energetic, with a desire to communicate and a distaste of 'trade secrets'; fairly manic...!...always learning and/but still hungry to know more; highly motivated; generous with time (but watch and control this); modest and sometimes worried enough about their own ability to want to continue to maintain sharpness; possessing high levels of stamina and concentration; good natural teaching psychology; able to temper expectations; educational vision; remembering how difficult it is to begin; *self-*motivation.

Unsuccessful tutors: – there aren't that many because most of them don't really start, but there are unhappy ones – lazy, looking for easy ways to teach, standing still, looking back rather than forward, viewing tuition as a second option because something else didn't work out, unwilling to admit they don't know it all (who does? A brain-dead person might pretend), putting little or nothing into teaching other than just enough time.

BEGINNING

The steps you need to take will depend on where you are now on your journey to become a full-time tutor. Are you a complete novice (as far as teaching goes) or a 'rookie', experienced, already part-time, side-stepping from somewhere else in the industry or from another teaching career?

Whatever your answer, there may be new skills you will need to acquire as well as old ones you can use or adapt. Even so, exploring the job from the ground up will ensure that you don't miss something important – rather in the way you might approach initial lessons with an experienced player.

Picking brains: The best way of finding out is to talk to...tutors! This booklet is just a start and can't answer questions for every circumstance. Most genuine tutors will be happy to tell you anything you wish to know about what they do, how they do it, as well as the bits of the music world they know about. This can be done as part of a lesson if you're a regular student or you could book some special time: often this kind of session needs to be open-ended, for a set fee or with the fee calculated after the session has closed – this way you can relax and ask all you need to know and/or draw the session to a close when you're running out of money! The best advice I've had was from people who had been there and done it. Remember that it is really important to work out what you *don't* want as soon as you can: talking to those with experience can save you heartache...and cash.

You need a combination of experience, qualifications and contacts (each one of these can lead to the others). The main point is to aim at what you want to do and try to take the right route now. There is plenty of help and good advice out there these days. It's also a good idea not to limit your options *too* much too early (if ever – this industry changes and that's part of what keeps it going).

Qualify: If you haven't already and have little in the way of direct experience, you need to address this. It is quite competitive out there. Even if the first decade of the 21st century looks like a good time to be teaching guitar, the best work will still go to the best tutors. Further education is an option if you're the right age to make that easy or you have enough savings to take time out to do this. If not, consider a part-time route: lessons with a private tutor are almost certainly the most flexible option.

Still at school? Are you studying for GCSE music? If it's still an option you're considering, do it. The skills you pick up will have surprising knock-on effects, even if you feel at the time that there seems little relevance. As a tutor, knowledge and understanding of school music exams can be valuable in helping your students who are also studying music at school. The same goes for 'A' level music.

Many non-classical students assume there will be nothing in it for them. Such exams are far more wide-ranging now, with most of the skills that you'll pick up being useful and also applicable to different forms of music. Much depends on the teacher you have at school or college, of course.

College courses can be quite practical; there is a big variety of approaches and some may leave you to your own devices a bit it seems. Check out first to see how 'hands-on' their philosophies are; ask what the placement rate is (of students leaving and going straight into their chosen work). Some college courses are modular – sign up for a diploma and you may end up staying a little longer to tack on a degree. You can usually opt for a course where you study your own instrument mainly.

Find out the entrance requirements. Generally you'll need a bare minimum of RGT/LCM Grade 4-6 standard. Aim at somewhere that seems keen to attract the right kind of students for this business, with courses geared to putting you into work in the industry, rather than just learning to be flash as some colleges seem to do.

Remember: you can take a music diploma through studying the grades – ask a tutor!

Advertising and PR: The best form of advertising is word-of-mouth. Your own satisfied students (past and present) will generate more extra work for you than all other forms of advertising together and this is where the vast majority (if not all) of an established tutor's new students will come from.

This is fine if you're a decent, established tutor of course!

For those just starting out or perhaps taking the plunge from part-time to full-time, then some form of advertising drive is necessary. The local newspaper can be cost-effective: it's quick, simple and you may be able to persuade them that a new, or expanding, tuition business is good news so have a one-off editorial into the bargain, perhaps even with a photograph of you in your teaching studio.

Shop locally! Keeping friendly with your music (and other) shops can pay dividends.

Putting cards in newsagents and music shops (sometimes there's a small weekly charge) can be effective, but make the effort to think about what your card looks like – a hand-scribbled one will simply show how little you care. Business cards are cheap: have a good quantity of a decent design printed; locally: think about it! Make them clear and easy to understand. Some music shops may be happy to keep a pile by the till rather than just one on a notice board. Tip: having them printed both sides will avoid shops using them as free bits of card to write notes on!

Door-to-door leaflets have been effective for some, if you don't mind the leg-work or the possible poor hit rate.

Belonging to a professional body can help advertise: most produce a directory or a list of their tutors on the internet.

Cyberspace is obviously effective but also a minefield. Your own simple website is probably best. There are many people out there asking for fees to increase your business via their internet schemes: some are good; some don't seem to know, or maybe care, what they're doing beyond taking your money. Checking them out is easy: contact a tutor who is already using the service to see how worthwhile it is. New sites usually offer free advertising initially, introducing fees when they're up-and-running, giving you the chance to see if it works for you.

National advertising is available through specialist magazines and journals. This tends to be pricey (but good deals can often be had by haggling) and you will obviously be getting to a large percentage of potential customers for whom you'll just be too far away, but this form of PR is probably good for your 'street cred' if such things bother you. On the other hand, just one good response and an advert pays for itself fairly quickly – always do this kind of calculation when considering advertising.

A word of warning: once it looks like you're up for some serious PR, you will be bombarded with calls offering you advertising space of one sort and another, usually from trained sales people who can be willing to use a variety of means in their attempts to be very persuasive. Be prepared!

Your own gigs will raise your profile and in effect promote you as a tutor. You could even organize self-promoted show-case gigs where the publicity points at you as a tutor. Remember that what most people want from a teacher is approachability rather than a guitar god who can play so many zillion notes a minute but who looks like he or she wouldn't give the time of day to mere mortals.

One very effective way of gaining new students while working is through self-organized workshops. These can be short or half-day or whole-day one-offs or offered as courses over several weeks. Set them up so that the timings appeal to your market (school holiday daytimes for children; evenings or weekends for adults) and be very clear in your advertising exactly what you propose to do. Keep it simple offering definite, realistic expectations. If the workshops go well and people like you, you're bound to have some book up for subsequent lessons. This is a whole subject really: as with the rest of this book, we're only dealing with ideas, simple considerations and principles here.

Planning and preparation

Making and keeping records: essential; there is no substitute and playing catch-up later will probably be a nightmare.

My advice is to make and maintain records always, even if you don't feel this is necessary now (after all, we could all keep track of a small handful of students who come for lessons every week). Unless you have the most extraordinary short-term and long-term recall you will need to refer to notes of past lessons, progress, exam passes, problematic issues, preferences and requests. Someone will mention on their first lesson "one day I'd like to be able to play…" and name a piece. It'll make them and you feel good if in a few weeks or months they arrive at a lesson with that same tune on the music stand and you know that they are by then able to tackle it. I've had instances of students contacting me many years after their last lesson and asking if I remember what they were studying then – if I can't, I do know I have a record.

If a student stays with you for many years (very likely indeed if you're good at the job and they like you), you can keep a really good eye on their progress while ensuring that you don't – after some years and several hundred tunes perhaps – repeat something accidentally! A trivial note, but I'm often asked: "when was my first lesson?"…

Perhaps this is as good a place as any to consider **what we, as music tutors, actually do**…

When filling out those pesky forms — such as insurance companies like to give us and they ask what you do — the title of the job is easy but they often go on to ask then for a description. I used to do my best in the tiny space they give but now simply write "pass on knowledge". This for me is the very basic tangible thing I begin doing with any student. If I said that was all I had been given by the teacher who has meant the most to me then I would have barely scratched the surface of his legacy to me.

A good tutor will: offer guidance; constantly give encouragement as well as permission to the student to become the musician they are capable of being; engage in realistic but energetic confidence-building which can continue long after lessons have ceased; give research tips (oh, and some! - I speak from experience both as a tutor and student); promote understanding over memorizing; and inspire enthusiasm. All of this needs an ability to communicate. There is no standard way of doing this: different students learn in different ways and respond to different methods. **Perhaps the greatest skill a decent tutor will possess is the ability to latch on and adapt quickly to how each individual learns best.**

NLP may help you in learning how students learn - and, if this is new to you, remember that a good tutor is a constant student too!

Initial lessons can often be the most awkward, possibly the *only* really tricky one, for you *and* the student. Many things are happening in a short space of time: you are assessing each other on different levels, in different ways, discovering if the chemistry and mutual trust necessary for a good learning and mentoring environment are there to build on. Allow the student to input as many of their wishes, aspirations, doubts, fears and previous knowledge as possible. Make it clear what kind of tutor you are, what you can and can't do. Being fairly formal at the start will often ease the situation and provides an excellent start; you can lighten up and adapt to each of your students' styles as you get to know each other, but don't be officious or patronizing.

Bear in mind that for many it's a hobby, pastime, a stress-buster or relaxation. Avoid making it hard work: find out how much your student wants to put in before you decide how hard to push.

A quick word about new students: some give up soon for several reasons, usually that they discover that it is going to require more work than they thought; many will stick at it for a fair time, although progress is rarely a simple curve and has many peaks, troughs and points of plateau; slower learners can be very rewarding long-term as pennies drop, making weeks or months of hard slog suddenly very worthwhile, with apparently instant, sudden extensions to their understanding and knowledge often then being well retained (unlike some quicker learners and wizz-kids who forget as fast as they remember or become complacent because they think they find it easy so end up learning slower).

No tutor, no-*one*, knows it all. Learn to use the expression: "I don't know but I'll find out" at all the appropriate times. Never offer bullshit instead. If we've learned (of course we have) then we all have people we can ask. This vast network is what it's all about.

Set-up – what do you offer? Where do you or where are you going to teach? Perhaps you're thinking of teaching at home or already do so and are considering adding something a bit more purpose-built to your property or acquiring premises away from home. There are pros and cons to all of the options of course. The *Back-to-back Breadwinning* chapter (see page 35) includes a few others by looking further afield.

Working in your home

Pros:

You don't have to 'go' to work!
Easy to keep all your reference material to hand.
No need for extra phone, heat, light supply...
Minimal extra overheads.
Convenient and secure.

Cons:

If you work at home you're always at work!
Students know where you live – some will therefore expect you always to be there and be on hand so your privacy can disappear.
Other people in your house may need to work round your tuition hours; if not, your teaching practice may seem a little unprofessional.
You'll 'lose' part of your home (as a home).
You may find, in some areas, that you have to satisfy certain local government regulations.

Working in a purpose-built studio at home

Pros:

You don't have far to go to work! You don't have far to go home!
Your extra phone, heat and light supplies are easy to manage.
No extra ongoing rent.
Convenient.
If self contained you can get away from it to a degree and it doesn't disrupt the household.
Professional presentation.

Cons:

If you work from home you're always at work!
Students know where you live – some will therefore expect you always to be there and be on hand so your privacy can disappear.
You may find, in some areas, that you have to satisfy certain local government regulations.
Cost of providing or converting and maintaining the room or building.
Security and insurance if it's a free-standing building.

Other general pros and cons to private teaching include:

Waiting room? Are you going to provide somewhere or cope with those students who arrive early (and those that hang about after lessons, perhaps holding up the next student)?

Sound-proofing – why? Is it to keep the sound in (unlikely unless you're looking to do yourself and your students some ear damage or have seriously thin walls or are trying to placate a fussy neighbour)? Or is it to keep outside sounds from disrupting the lesson? How much sound-proofing are you likely to need? Does it need to be structural and permanent or will temporary measures (screens) do the job? It's worth doing it properly from the outset.

Distractions: as few as possible is ideal of course; try not to have a phone in your tuition area, nor people passing through; keep it professional looking; items in your teaching space should relate to the job at hand.

Gear – what are you going to provide? It's reasonable to supply amps and cables. It's also possible of course to supply instruments (but your students will be better off taking lessons with their own) – you may wish to have a studio spare of each instrument type you teach for odd occasions when it's necessary or convenient.

Cigarettes, alcohol, garlic, socks, trainers…and any other types of B.O. or any kind of 'O.' (the sweat generated in an intense lesson can be quite a killer to walk into from the fresh air outside!) – these are all atmospheres that you must contend with at some time, perhaps daily. First try to ensure that you are not the cause. Back-to-back tuition means that any such situation in one lesson can't be dealt with before the next.

Think about air extraction (usually quite simple to have installed) or air conditioning (sometimes not so simple, especially in sound-proof environments).

Safety policy and windows: very serious issues can arise from teaching children one-to-one with no-one else present during the lesson.

One slight unfounded accusation, or even a comment which could be misunderstood, could ruin you at least professionally and cause emotional turmoil. Parents or guardians with difficult children can offer to sit in with them – for your sake at least as much as their own. Although most children learn better without another person present, in some cases it is advisable so be open to this extra supervision. Having at least one large public window in your teaching room is sensible – any less will leave you very vulnerable. This is a very important issue which needs serious consideration.

Clock/watch: you will need to keep track of time.

Setting up a clock behind where your students sit (or stand?!) will mean you can do this subtly while they are not distracted by how much time has passed.

Public Liability: it is advisable to have some insurance cover for this. If you work in the public sector it will often be imperative.

Talking of which…it is worth your while to consider joining the **Musicians' Union**. Some feel political about this, some don't but there is no doubt that our Union is exactly what it says on the tin. What you can offer the Union (other than your annual sub) is up to you; there is plenty in the Union for you when you need it, not the least of which is well negotiated public liability insurance. I have my own issues about some of the ways the Union is run (so am not trying to sell anything to you for any of the wrong reasons) but I recommend being a member. The solidarity is important too. Subs are based, very fairly, on how much you earn as a musician.

There are other professional bodies such as the RGT, NAME, EGTA – it's not appropriate to run through the lot here. Most will offer some kind of benefit, probably less tangible than those of the MU, but help towards your CPD, informative newsletters and so on can all add up to make you a better tutor. You may be amazed to find how soon the sub seems to pay for itself – sometimes with just one piece of invaluable information or an elusive contact.

Reference books: you can't have too many; the world never stands still so don't go on using just those that you learned with – keep up to date. See the last section for a selection, but don't be limited: stay always on the look-out for good reference material.

Lessons – duration? Most tutors offer in blocks of ½ hour – this equates roughly to how long it's estimated that most people can concentrate sensibly. Shorter lessons are suitable for the very young, those with concentration difficulties etc. Longer lessons are often appropriate for adults, especially those studying at a high level. Take care to break the lessons up, even engineering a short relaxed conversation every now and then to refresh or by altering the subject matter at sensible intervals.

Do you wish to teach back-to-back or not? This can depend on your circumstances, studio set-up or other, sometimes personal, considerations. I dislike back-to-back private music lessons on the whole for many reasons so try to build a 10 or 15 minute 'buffer' between lessons. This time is my time, although it often gets eaten up: parents come and chat, maybe a student arrives very early, some people seem not to be able to leave until the next person enters the room…

…however it's used, it's actually at your cost. It helps me rest easy that every student does get their full lesson time (and gives me spaces where I can make up timing errors or to just finish a subject properly without ruining the beginning of another student's lesson). You'll have plenty of hours for which you don't get paid in preparing lessons, researching, maintaining equipment, doing your paperwork. Those gaps between lessons just add to the time you *give* to the job. If this is likely to annoy you, get to you and chew you up, then organize your diary carefully...or find other work.

This booklet is about being a guitar tutor. We tend to polarize and specialize more with the years. In my case, I now teach less and less pure guitar. Improvisation, theory, composition, as well as tuition as a subject in itself, the psychology that goes with that and general musicianship (guitar-based or not) all make up the bigger part of my working day. It's worth bearing in mind these allied subjects from the beginning as they may be areas in which you already have a special interest or some expertise. Theory, improvisation, sight reading and song-writing are all popular subjects in their own right; many technically decent guitar players need to hone these skills and will therefore seek specialized lessons. One guitar teacher I know even used to offer tuition in style, although how much demand there is for advice in what type of boots to wear for successful goth-metal or the ideal hair-cut for a Dowland recital – I wouldn't know! Oh dear, this book has let somebody down...

Diversification has been a buzz-word in agriculture for years now. Guitar tutors should consider it too. Can you (do you *want* to) take on repairs and set-ups? I always did my own; word got round and I started doing it for students, then being asked by folks who heard on the grapevine to the point where it drove me nuts (I never really enjoyed it and hadn't intended it should become part of my business).

So be careful what you begin to undertake.

Is there a local music retailer? If not, offering a selection of strings and music books for sale could help your students and add a retail dimension to your tuition practice – or it could become a pain you wish you'd never started. Think about it and as many of the implications as you can; talk to those who have been there.

Your geographical area: consider the demography. Your consideration here is simple: will your chosen catchment area support a full-time guitar tutor (for whatever reasons)?

Experience: how will your background help (or even hinder) you? The answers can be surprising, usually surprisingly positive if you know how to look.

Wait – don't start teaching just yet – read the next short chapter!

BUSINESS

You are one. You are a business. As a tutor you cannot hide behind 'product' or some corporate image. You are selling yourself and your time – that's all you have to sell.

You may have one or two issues on how you view that. You may think you only sell your time. This is pretty much how I see it. Or you might feel that you sell yourself, or that you sell both these rather woolly concepts (this is probably the most realistic). Whatever, the business is you.

Charges – per…? This is always a problem when you start (either from scratch or step up to full time) as, once you've set your fees, changing them in any dramatic way can be tricky. First consider your lessons – how long are they? This seems a silly question but, if you are the kind of tutor that gives fairly open-ended lessons, you may wish to charge by the lesson. This is a bit like the opposite of a blank cheque – you will need to know how to terminate lessons when it suits you. The old 'cross my palm with silver' method is unlikely to work: a friend tried it. We all feel awkward sometimes as we know that some people can afford more than others. Means-testing is impractical. My friend asked clients to leave what they felt her time was worth. I could have predicted the results: on the whole, those who were well off left much less than her minimum rate payments; those who couldn't really afford to generally gave more than had she asked for the going rate!

Many music teachers feel strongly about their role and their responsibility: being able to pass on knowledge and skills while encouraging someone to learn and develop as a musician is a wonderful privilege - as well as being intensive work! This can make us feel that we might be happy to do this anyway if someone just paid the rent/mortgage, fed and watered and clothed us – 'will work for gas, food, lodging'. Putting a price on what we do can be hard, but it's necessary.

After years of heart-searching and pocket-searching, my own method is to charge a very transparent hourly rate (which I extend to cover everything that I do: tuition, composition, projects, work shopping, consultancy, gigging, recordings and session work – all from when I leave home to when I get back). This I modify by a form of loyalty discount. When I put my fees up (not every year and not automatically, just when I think it's fair or necessary) clients that I count as 'old-timers' are either immune to this or benefit from a smaller increase. I'm open about this to new customers too so they know why some others may pay less - and how they may be in the same situation in the future. It works well for me, but may not suit you.

Contracts: the MU can supply sample contracts for you to use or base yours on. Many tutors use them and have clauses stipulating that a whole term's lesson must be paid for as notice of termination etc. Music lessons to me are, above all, about mutual trust. I have never issued any written form of contract. The list of bad debts owing to me can be counted on the fingers of one hand. If you have a contract and someone defaults, will you chase it up? If the answer is 'yes', then issue contracts and run your business well: you'll be paid twice for some hours and sometimes be paid for not working at all. If the answer is 'no', why bother? In either case, be prepared to pay for, or work for, your business principles.

Sliding scale: some tutors work out fees by beginning with a basic (MU minimum? Basic school rate?) then add for the extras they offer – purpose built studio, recording lessons for students to listen back to later at home, loaning gear, providing music and other materials, experience, qualifications, and so on.

Contact time: this is the time you spend actively involved with students. Your fee will have to cover a lot more time than this.

What are you selling? If at all, how can we liken the teaching of music to other trades, professions and industries? Just food for thought...

Missed lessons – what are you going to do if and when your students just don't turn up, or perhaps are polite enough to cancel a lesson...2 minutes before it's due to begin? You can't resell it. You need a policy. It can be rigid or flexible. I'm lenient with genuine people, but it can be really annoying when...well...beware the...

...Holidays – do you want to teach during this season of chaos when more students change lesson times than don't, plenty forget to arrive at all, parents manage to lose children or bring them an hour late because they can't quite recall the lesson time even though it's been the same time on the same weekday for five years (they're busy parents with busy kids: those who bring their children for lessons are the good, supportive ones – don't be hard on them) - and you do need to be understanding and pleasant, even if you're also quite firm: they are your customers and the reason you are able to eat...

...so...when do *you* take ...

Time off? My wife saw this heading and said "what's that?"...

Most of us seem to take the attitude of grabbing the work while it's there – after all, tomorrow's popular instrument could suddenly turn out to be the ophicleide or the harp. Of course that is unlikely (!) but most tutors are prepared to work hard, long and unsociable hours, for many reasons. It goes with the territory of course but is also a reflection of the kind person that makes a decent teacher.

I'm probably the worst person on the planet to tell you to take time out, self-motivation being one of my stronger 'skills', but do try to allow yourself some time: it could be regular (a day a week) or just making sure you take some decent breaks. It benefits you, the business and everyone around you, ensuring you'll be regenerated.

Consider the hours you'd like to keep: being a night-owl suits private tuition pretty well. There are students who will want lessons during the day but the most popular time will be from about 3.30pm until 8pm (you may find you could probably sell this time several times over), but you'll also have those willing to study late or shift workers, allowing you to teach anywhere in the 24-hour clock. Most people suffer some sort of energy-dip (often around 4.30pm) – if there are times during which you don't function well, write them out of your available teaching diary.

Enforced time away from work is a different matter: you may feel fit or bullet-proof but you need to think about some sickness cover. There are plenty of companies willing to quote you for this (rest assured you pay a price that means they make the money with virtually no risk) – study what's on offer carefully to make sure it suits. I've paid into various schemes in the past but now belong to a Friendly Society and feel I have the best deal. If you're not sure, take advice: try to seek it from a tutor who has had to use the cover.

Copyright and photocopies: be careful; copies for page turns and to write on when studying to avoid ruining a book are acceptable perhaps but the law is there to protect creative people.

It's a powerful law and not worth messing with, besides the moral issue.

You're running a business: you'll need to keep good accurate **accounts** in decent order; also helps you when you need to research an old invoice or record of something; and if you don't then you're inviting the tax office to estimate your tax liability for you - and that's unlikely to be less than reality! NI (National Insurance) – find out what you have to pay and pay it. This isn't PAYE: no one is going to do this for you. Don't delay. A good accountant with an understanding of the music industry will be well worth employing: keep nice clear records, do as much of your own book-keeping as possible (or use a book-keeper for this work – cheaper than letting an accountant do it) and your accounts bill will be kept to a minimum.

Declare it all? I believe it's a good thing to do: it helps you see exactly how well your business is doing (or not), where your expenses are and how they relate to your earnings; besides, there is nothing wrong with fair taxation – it'd be nice if the proceeds were spent with more wisdom and care!

Car insurance! This needs mentioning: when enquiring for a quotation if you say you're a musician some companies won't even quote – shop around, tell them you're a music teacher. A handful of insurance firms will help. Again this is the kind of thing the Musicians' Union are able to help with if you are a member.

BACK-TO-BACK BREADWINNING!

Continuation: doing the job

Invest: there is no substitute for putting your time, energy, resources and learning into your tuition business. Investing in it will keep it vibrant. Starving it will help it die.

Formality: remember to be professional at all times; your students can become good friends but they are still paying you for a service so a lesson should remain that.

Chat before or after; don't feel you can munch on a roll during a lesson just because you've got to know someone well - letting that stomach rumble is a more professional option!

Parents: they are your customers too - they pay! Keep them in touch. Your duty of care as a tutor is different for parent and child: their child is your student, so this is where they pay you to focus and therefore your primary concern. I put the child first and tell the parents this: an overbearing or negative parent (or tutor!) can ruin a child's musicality for life. It's a responsibility to be taken seriously, although the lessons should be fun.

You may wish to branch out and extend your business. We are really concerned here with private guitar tuition. Other options, however, include: youth clubs; music shops; schools – private or state; colleges – including evening classes. You may prefer to consider travelling to students' homes as an extension to your tuition from home, although you will need to plan and cost this carefully, taking time and motoring costs into consideration, something which may mean your fees end up at an off-putting level.

There are allied subjects within teaching which may

help you expand on the perceptions of what you do as a guitar tutor. If you are any good at the job you are essentially a music teacher, so other aspects of being a guitarist (or a musician who operates a guitar) will be part of what you can offer: sight reading, theory, improvisation, composition, advice to young bands, even styling and stage presence!

Repairs and set-ups are also a possible add-on. Many teachers do their own and so acquire these sought-after skills.

CRB checks: it's a basic assurance to parents, even if they are only really worth as much as an MOT. Any employer will have to (or should) get your CRB check done. If you've not worked for an authority, youth club or similar, you can apply to have a simple one done yourself. It takes time and costs money but is worthwhile, if not essential. Whoever starts the process, you ultimately retain the paperwork for this; authorities etc just need to see it. Contact your local police HQ if you need advice.

Exams: there are currently quite a number of exam boards to choose from: ABRSM, Trinity Guildhall, LCM, Victoria are just some. Attendance, and the support this brings, at your students' exams can help them enormously and contribute to how they feel about you as a caring teacher. It is a dead loss financially as you'll not get paid, cancel lessons to be there and probably have to travel – but the 'cuddle' factor is well worthwhile and you may help them get slightly better results or be there to save an exam-threatening situation such as a broken string or tuning problem. Taking the bigger picture is always worthwhile and pays off – unless your intention is only to be a guitar tutor for five minutes, in which case why have you read this far?!

UCAS – inform your students about the value of

higher grade exams towards their UCAS points. There are even schools and colleges that seem not to know about this. More detailed information can be found from exam board websites, such as LCM or ABRSM.

Concerts: students often lack the opportunity to play in public or in ensembles. Organizing gigs for them to perform in front of a supportive audience of friends, relations and other students is an effective way of starting or boosting their confidence, giving them valuable experience, helping them to meet other players and perhaps kick-starting further performance opportunities.

Colleagues: keep in touch. Guitar tuition can be an oddly lonesome career – unless you work in schools (sometimes even if you do) there is no common room time. Take time to have a coffee or beer with guitar (and other instrumental) tutors: it'll do everyone some good.

Professional advice: whether this is from an accountant or mentor it is well worth paying for if you feel the need. Asking is always better than wondering or guessing.

Your area: make local knowledge a priority. Understanding your patch including the state of general education and the wider music scene will ensure you don't become an island or overlook something which could be vital information for your business.

BEYOND?

Building on your own development

Invest: continue to invest in time and resources. It's like breathing.

Learn: none of us will ever know it all; this is an infinite subject. Stop learning and it will show. The symptoms are: feeling tired of the job; the days dragging; students losing interest. If you don't *feel* like learning more, perhaps you're tired of the job or music itself? Perhaps you need a break? Or just a refresher course of some kind?

Learn about the ways we learn – it could be argued that this is the biggest part of the job. There are many schools of thought on this: bookshops, libraries and the internet will be full of information. Use your own experience and common sense while evaluating theories: don't start to use methods unless you understand them. Learn to know when to check out or distrust glib generalizations – there are some in this booklet, intended only to get you thinking in the right direction. Always try things out for yourself. NLP is a current 'buzz' acronym. Don't know what it stands for? Guess what my advice might be: find out! That's a fundamental part of being a teacher: being able to find out. If you can't or don't enjoy doing this, then maybe being a tutor is not for you.

Research outside your subject.

Not all good advice appropriate to guitar tutors is found in resources concerning guitar tuition or even music. Much of the best source material I've found has been in other fields. Here's an example: while looking into the techniques and the psychology for good sight reading I tried to find analogies elsewhere. One was rock climbing, in particular climbing without ropes.

The similarity may not be clear at first but a climber attempting a route for the first time has a job to do rather like a musician reading a piece for the first time. If the climber makes a serious error he or she might die – should be some handy advice here then! Guitarists are not staring at a fatal outcome as a result of sight reading mistakes but some knowledge of how climbers avoid going wrong should help. A couple of books on power rock climbing proved more useful than many of the volumes on sight reading I had read. A fair amount of research had discovered something the brain does when learning…

Engrams: this is a term for what happens when the brain learns small muscle memories. Don't get this confused with the same word as used in Dianetics – it's not the same at all! In short the brain can learn a muscle memory for *types* of move. So we can use this to help us acquire better reading skills even when dealing with music that is new to us, just as climbers use information about the types of move that they may encounter on new routes.

Therefore, what appears new to us may well possess some form of familiarity. I'm not doing the subject justice here of course; just attempting to illustrate how we can benefit from researching outside our chosen subject.

CPD is another big buzz acronym – most music tutors I know see it as part of their job; other trades and professions look on it as unnecessary or a chore, the complaints of the brain-dead. There is very little available CPD specifically for guitar tutors.

One of the few exceptions is the annual RGT conference.

Held every Autumn, it is open to non-registered tutors. Choice of seminars is wide (you won't be able to attend them all as many run concurrently) although those aimed at higher levels (as with most available learning opportunities for tutors) are fewer. There is not usually a great deal of warning either and a London venue, generally on a Sunday, won't suit everyone.

Other aspects to be considered:

Books, journals and magazines help you keep up to date as well as widening your knowledge.

Regular reviews for your students and self are important: reviewing students' progress can be done by you without their knowledge (just reading back through the lesson notes helps you keep in touch with their progress and aspirations) or with them. Re-assessing their aims after an exam can be helpful for instance. Reviewing yourself takes a little more effort as it's too easy just to plough on sometimes. Booking up for a specialist course or taking some lessons in the form of advanced guidance, with a teacher who has specialist knowledge or more experience, are two ways of ensuring you take stock.

Further education; you may well be involved with sending students on into further education, formal or otherwise; part of this process might take the form of careers advice (there are many of us who wish we'd received better...or just any). This is a very responsible part of being a tutor as advising a student on the best path forward, a suitable music diploma, college or university course can affect somebody's life in many ways. Don't be glib and don't guess.

Specialities, or music as something else: it's well known that music makes good therapy, however much some of us tend to be suspicious of the word. As music tutors we can also help behaviour problems, give those with learning difficulties some confidence and many other less tangible 'spin-offs' from the music learning environment, especially on a one-to-one basis. Unless you are otherwise qualified ensure that the person who is hiring you is aware that what you are giving is music lessons, whatever the 'ulterior motive' may be. Don't pretend to be a therapist if you're not one!

Assessments: sometimes someone wants to know what level they are; perhaps a less experienced tutor needs some help in assessing a new or tricky student; exam candidates like to take a mock exam with a tutor they don't know prior to an exam session.

If you're able to offer these services they can be a valuable addition to your tuition business. Remember you may wish to be assessed yourself, perhaps for suitable further training.

Side steps: not a chromatic move! Our careers aren't always mapped out by our wishes. My osteopath passed on some advice he once received: we get the clients we deserve!

This means that your clients often start to tell you what your strengths are and your career therefore could make moves in directions you had not expected nor specifically trained for: it was certainly not something I'd aimed at but my own tuition now centres on teaching tutors, those who are training to be tutors and professionals.

For many years I've been hearing that I am a 'theory expert' although I did not promote myself as such. Through being a composer, unexpectedly allied to my interest in special needs children and adults, I also do a lot of work as a project leader. This was not a deliberate career move. It happened by being defined by those who were hiring me. It comes about as an accident of our training, passions and skills; we are not always the best placed people to see this clearly...
...so listen.

Appendices

BACK-UP

Support and resources

Picking brains: guitar teaching can be a lonely business. There is no common room for private guitar tutors to share a coffee and a chat. Guitars don't get much chance to play in ensembles, outside small bands and groups, so there's little or no orchestra experience, nor the chance to meet with other tutors and musicians at those kinds of events.

It's important that we interact with colleagues. We all have specialist skills and knowledge.

Picking brains and sharing information has a greater purpose than just spreading this know-how.

Talk to people! Experienced musicians are usually happy to tell interested students anything they wish to know about what they do, how they do it, etc and the bits of the music world they know about. The best advice I've had was from people who had been there and done it. Likewise I'm always happy to pass on knowledge and advice to any of my students who ask.

Colleagues are not rivals or competitors: we're all in the same business and helping each other will make the business better. Students will appreciate this and so will you. All the *successful* music tutors as well as music retailers that I know get on well with other tutors and shops. Unless you want to be a human and professional island (with all the problems that will encourage) don't shut yourself off from one of our best assets - our colleagues.

Insurance, public liability, the Musicians' Union, the Registry of Guitar Tutors and other bodies have all been mentioned (as have resources such as journals and books). Join in, use them, help out. Give the knowledge you have; seek out and accept the knowledge others have to give.

BALANCING BUSY-NESS

(Having a Life - or not)

I've thought long and hard about this and this is where whatever expertise I have runs out.

Other than those odd tips (few of which I listen to myself) that I've offered in previous pages, I'm definitely not the right person to look to for advice here.

The Musicians' Union runs occasional courses or seminars on this subject. I have attended one and it helps you look at yourself. This is what you have to do: assess. If you are the sort of person who lives on drive then perhaps you don't need balance.

We all need to recharge and in teaching we tend to give out more than we get back, at least for some of the time.

The balance I find is the knowledge that this is vocational: I do it because I want to. If I wake up one day and I really don't want to teach that day I can just phone round and cancel the lessons in the diary. It's unlikely it'll happen and I'd have to suffer the consequences of course but just the knowledge that this is my business to run how I wish (rather than that feeling most of us have that our diaries are running us!) is enough for me to feel each day that I do this through some sort of choice.

Over the page I've put down a couple of typical weeks in a guitar tutor's working life.

It doesn't include those occasional necessaries such as visiting music shops, ordering music and so on, nor special one-offs such as obtaining training, nor simple daily essentials, nor other frequent events in a musician's life like gigs.

Here are a couple of samples of real weeks in the life of a full-time guitar tutor

The first is a typical pure tuition week, with no 'extras' of any kind:

Monday:
10am: prepare lessons with coffee and answer student
    phone calls and emails
12 noon: lesson to a professional until 2.30pm (with
    tea!)
2.30-3pm: write up lesson notes and study notes for
    next lessons
3pm: eat
3.30pm: more lesson preparation
4.30pm: teach (hour and half-hour lessons) until 10pm
10pm: write up lesson notes; answer student emails
10.30pm: eat
11.30pm: prepare lesson material

Tuesday:
10am: prepare lessons with coffee and answer student
    phone calls and emails
11.30am: teach until 12.30pm
12.30-3pm: time off
3pm: lesson preparation and study notes for next
    lessons
4.30pm: teach (hour and half-hour lessons) until 9pm
9pm: write up lesson notes
9.30pm: eat
10pm: meeting with colleague (and well-earned pint)
1.30am: prepare lesson material; answer student
    emails

Wednesday:

9.30am: prepare lessons with coffee and answer student phone calls and emails

10.45am: teach (hour and half-hour lessons) until 1.30pm

1.30pm: write up lesson notes

2pm: prepare lessons

3pm: eat

3.30pm: answer student phone calls

3.45pm: teach (hour and half-hour lessons) until 11pm

11pm: eat

11.30pm: write up lesson notes

Thursday:

9.30am: prepare lessons with coffee and answer student phone calls and emails

10.45am: teach (hour and half-hour lessons) until 2.30pm

2.30pm: eat

3pm: write up lesson notes

3.30pm: break until 4.30pm

4.30pm: teach (mainly hour lessons) until 10pm

10pm: eat

10.30pm: write up lesson notes; answer student emails

11pm: prepare lesson material

Friday:

10.30am: prepare lessons with coffee; answer student emails

11am: teach (half-hour and hour lessons) until 3.15pm

3.15pm: eat

4pm: teach until 6pm

6pm: answer student phone calls; prepare lessons

6.30pm: teach until 8.45pm

8.45pm: write up lesson notes

9.30pm: eat

10.30pm: prepare lessons material; answer student emails

Saturday:
10am: teach until 11.15;
write up lesson notes;
time off

Sunday: rehearsal and time off

and a more varied one:

Monday:
10am: prepare lessons with coffee; answer student emails
10.30am: until 12.30am: meeting with workshop client
12.30-3pm: write up workshop plans and contact colleagues verifying dates and availability etc
3pm: eat
3.30pm: prepare lessons
4.45pm: teach (hour and half-hour lessons) until 11pm
11pm: write up lesson notes; answer student emails
11.30pm: eat
12midnight: prepare lesson material

Tuesday:
10am: prepare lessons with coffee and answer student phone calls and emails
11.30am: teach until 12.30pm
12.30-3pm: lesson to professional, with a break for coffee
3pm: lesson preparation and study notes for next lessons
4.30pm: teach (hour and half-hour lessons) until 8.15pm

8.15pm: write up lesson notes

8.45pm: eat and relax

9.30pm: meeting with colleagues (and well-earned pint)

1.30am: prepare lesson material; answer student emails

Wednesday:

10am: prepare lessons with coffee and answer student phone calls

10.45am: teach (hour and half-hour lessons) until 1.30pm

1.30pm: write up lesson notes

2pm: prepare lessons; research workshop material

3pm: eat

3.30: answer student phone calls

3.45pm: teach (hour and half-hour lessons) until 10.30pm

10.30pm: write up lesson notes

11pm: eat; relax

12midnight prepare workshop material

Thursday:

9.30am: prepare lessons with coffee; answer student emails

10.45am: teach (hour and half-hour lessons) until 12.30pm

12.30pm: eat; write up lesson notes

1pm: travel to workshop venue

1.30pm: run workshop until 5pm

5pm: travel home

5.30pm: eat; answer student phone calls and emails; relax

7pm teach (half-hour and hour lessons) until 10pm

10pm: eat; write workshop report; answer student emails

10.30pm: meeting with workshop colleague

12midnight: prepare lesson material

Friday:

10.30am: prepare lessons with coffee; answer student emails

11am: teach (half-hour and hour lessons) until 12.15pm

12.15pm: write up lesson notes

1pm: prepare workshop material; eat

3.30pm: travel to workshop venue

5pm: run workshop briefing

6pm: run workshop teach until 9pm

9pm: workshop debriefing

9.30pm: travel home

10.30pm: eat; write workshop report

Saturday:

9.30am: prepare lessons

10am: teach until 11.15pm;

write up lesson notes;

time off

Sunday:

restring guitars;

running repairs;

answer student phone calls;

time off

BOOKS

This is not a bibliography, just a starting point for further research...

Joseph O'Connor
Not pulling strings : a book about instrumental teaching and music (Kahn and Averill)
Lots of common sense and plenty of info about NLP.

Lee F Ryan
The natural classical guitar (Kahn and Averill)
Not just for classical guitarists.
Excellent approach to great technique, posture, articulation, sound and mental attitude.

Fanny Waterman
On piano teaching and performing (Faber)
If you don't get something from this small booklet I would seriously question your musicianship.

Paul Harris
Improve your teaching (Faber)
Fabulous book: not big so you can read it quickly but there's a wealth of ideas here and sound advice from someone who knows his stuff.

Tony Skinner and Chaz Hart
...have written and edited books on sight reading, bass playing, lead improvisation, rhythm

playing and demo lessons published by RPL (publishing arm of RGT), all with years of solid and sound experience behind them.

Anthony Glise
Classical guitar Pedagogy: a handbook for teachers (Mel Bay)
Big book beautifully printed—which is what this wonderful work deserves.
Plenty for non-classical players in here.

T R Miles and John Westcombe
Music and Dyslexia: opening new doors (Whurr)
A lot of varied contributions make this book valuable.

George Odam
The sounding symbol (Nelson Thornes)
Wisdom from a very wise man.

Mark Stringer (ed)
The music teacher's handbook (Faber)
I found it a bit superficial. A good introduction and overview for the inexperienced tutor perhaps.

Gary Spruce
Teaching Music (Open University)
A standard text.

Paul Harris
The Music teacher's companion: a practical guide; international edition (ABRSM)
To me a far better book than the Faber handbook, covering similar ground although, again, experienced tutors may find it doesn't tell them anything new.

My advice: it's worth reading any book like this just in case...

ABRSM
All together: teaching music in groups (ABRSM)
Good advice on many aspects of group work.

Chris Philpott
Learning to teach music in the secondary school (Routledge)
Quite academic and maybe not of direct relevance to guitar tutors but good supplementary material.

Susan Hallam
Instrumental teaching: a practical guide (Heinemann)
Just what it says and well worth it.

Chris Philpott and Charles Plummeridge (ed)
Issues in music teaching (Routledge)
If you are looking to get in-depth on the subject, this is a serious book.

Caroline Sharp
Providing instrumental music tuition (NFED)
More general than nitty gritty. Could be useful background info for those involved with education authorities and schools.

Keith Swanwick
Teaching music musically (Routledge)
We all want to do this.

Common Approach (Faber)
Produced in modules by a team of experts. A bold attempt at a curriculum. Has sound guidance on progress and lesson preparation. Expensive to buy the whole package perhaps but you don't need it all. Every tutor should own the guitar sections, available separately. Invaluable for new tutors.

And: remember my mention of how much I learned from books on teaching rock climbing. Never close your mind - I've just picked up a great tuition tip from a book about Wittgenstein...

Finally:
If some of my tuition 'philosophy' has come through these pages I guess that's all well and good, although that was not the intention.

But I would like to finish this small book with the one idea that I carry with me each day:

Teach to make yourself redundant

Producing clones or technicians who can play something just because you have shown them exactly how to do it is not music teaching.

It might be harder work to make a proper job of it but it'll keep you fresh and satisfied for your whole career as well as giving great service to your students.

Beware the signs: do students end up sounding and playing like you, rather than like themselves? If so, step back and rethink.

Teach understanding, so that your students will be able to become musicians in their own right.

Lightning Source UK Ltd.
Milton Keynes UK
UKOW050908241011

180842UK00001B/102/A